Alaska Lessons

*Timeless Life Lessons from
America's Last Frontier*

By Jerry Ross

Ultimate Goal Publications
Jasonville, Indiana
www.stayinthecastle.com

Alaska Lessons

Table of Contents

Introduction		5
1.	Seward's Folly	7
2.	Fun Facts and Quotable Quotes	9
3.	Alaska's Greatest Treasure	11
4.	The Churches of Alaska	13
5.	Wolf Pelts	17
6.	The Steps of a Good Man	19
7.	Uniquely Fairbanks	21
8.	I Sought for a Man Among Them	23
9.	"I Hurt it Picking"	25
10.	Wife's Turn	27
11.	Kodiak Island	29
12.	Seward	33
13.	An Inconvenient Diagnosis	35
14.	St. Mary's	37
15.	Moose Hunting	39
16.	The Work of the Ministry	41
17.	Trophy Hunts	43
18.	The Yupik People	45
19.	The Darkness	47
20.	A Wednesday Night Charge	49
21.	The Last Frontier	51
22.	Wheels Up	55

Alaska: from the Aleut word, Alyeska. Its meaning?
"That which the sea breaks against."

Introduction

I'm going to blame Evangelist Joe Asbury for what has become my Alaska addiction. Joe is a good friend who still attends the church I pastor. He's slowed down some now, but used to travel and preach quite a bit. About twice a year, he would preach up in Alaska. One day, I asked him when his next trip to Alaska would be.

"Next spring. Why? You want to go?"

"Yes, I thought I would just tag along and carry your bags. I've never been to Alaska and I want to see it... if you don't mind?"

He told me he would set the dates and let me know. A few weeks later, he handed me a piece of paper with a list of five churches in Alaska and the dates we would be at each one.

"Here, Pastor. These are the churches where you are scheduled to preach."

I looked up, shocked. "What happened to me just carrying your bags?"

"I called the pastors and told them I was bringing my pastor with me this trip, and they want you to preach. So, there's your schedule." He gave me a wry smile and walked away.

We had a wonderful trip. I preached in several churches in and around Anchorage and one church in Fairbanks. When I came back, my wife asked me what I thought of our 49th state.

"If I had gone to Alaska when I was 20 years old, I never would have come back."

I still believe that. On that first trip up there, I was 56 years of age. I have been back four times since then — three "white Alaska" trips and two during the summer. I am 62 years of age at the writing of this book, and it is a bit late to consider uprooting and relocating our lives. But every time I've gone to Alaska, on the flight back home, I've found myself planning how to get back.

Alaska is a wonderful state with wonderful people. The lessons I learned came from asking questions, listening, observing, rolling up my sleeves, and getting involved. My hope is that you find enjoyment and benefit from reading this book. So, let me carry your bags, as we travel together to *the last frontier*.

Dedicated to
Tim and De Etta Page
Faithful, Humble, Wonderful Servants of God
Hoosiers by Birth, Alaskans by Choice

CHAPTER ONE

Seward's Folly

"The best way to predict the future is to create it."
— William H. Seward

Before visiting a new part of the world for the first time, I always read up on it. Prior to my first visit to Alaska, I read five books about this amazing land. Since then I have read another dozen or so — books on its history; the gold rush; hunting, fishing, trapping stories; bush pilot adventures; homesteader tales; and accounts of the famed Iditarod. I have also read extensively about the people groups who are native to this land. The facts and stories gleaned from these books have enriched my visits to this incredible, vast treasure... a treasure our country purchased for two pennies an acre!

In 1741, Vitus Bering led an expedition that secured Alaska as a Russian territory. The czar sent fur trappers but few stayed. During the 18th and 19th centuries, there were never more than a couple of hundred Russians living in Alaska at any one time.

After America's Civil War, U.S. Secretary of State William H. Seward began negotiating with his Russian counterparts for the acquisition of Alaska. He eventually signed an agreement with Russia for the purchase of Alaska for 7.2 million dollars to be paid in gold. Despite the microscopic price of two cents an acre, the purchase was ridiculed by the American media as well as many prominent Congressmen of the day. Tagged as "Seward's Folly," "Seward's Icebox," and President Andrew Johnson's "Polar Bear Garden", a battle raged over the ratification of the agreement. Finally, on April 9, 1867, the purchase was sanctioned and the United States formally took possession on October 18th of the same year at a flag-changing ceremony in Sitka.

What some deemed *folly* became the greatest land acquisition in our nation's history. So what exactly did we get for this bargain-basement deal?

*ALASKA, our future 49th State.

*375 million acres (twice the size of Texas).

*More than 3000 rivers and 3 million lakes.

*17 of the 20 tallest peaks in North America, including the

highest — Mount Denali at 20,306 feet above sea level.

*100 volcanoes and volcanic fields.

*More coastline than what we already had combined.

*Vast reserves of coal, oil, natural gas, zinc, and lumber. (According to the Alaska Department of Natural Resources Division of Oil and Gas, in May of 2010 there were 19.2 million barrels of oil produced as well as 31.3 billion cubic feet of natural gas.)

*A promise-land for commercial and recreational fishing.

*An Edenic paradise for wildlife including grizzly bears, black bears, polar bears, brown bears (70% of the North American population), caribou, mountain goat, Dall sheep, bison, wolves, foxes, otters, beavers, and — most famously — the Alaskan moose.

Besides its vastness and natural resources, this land purchase has also bequeathed America with one of the most beautiful winter playgrounds on the planet. Tourists come from around the world to fish and hunt, to ski and snowmobile, to hike and camp, to fly and hang-glide, and just to relax and enjoy the majestic beauty. They come by car, plane, motorcycle, train, motorcoach, and cruise ship.

The tourism industry creates one in ten jobs in Alaska. Visitors spend $2.2 billion annually which helps support the local businesses, restaurants, and outfitters. One in three Alaska visitors are repeat travelers to the state. Well, I definitely became one of those!

The best way to educate yourself about this wonderful state is to read. Here are some books I have read and can recommend:

* *Alaska, Our Northern Wonderland* by Frank Carpenter
* *Hunting Alaska's Far Places* by Jim Rearden
* *One Man's Wilderness* by Sam Keith
* *Alaska* by James A. Michener
* *81 Days Below Zero* by Brian Murphy
* *Klondike Fever* by Pierre Berton

Seward's folly? It may have seemed like it to some at the time, but in telescopic hindsight, with a background of dancing Northern Lights, I see it differently. I think God used William H. Seward to bless America. Because all Americans, every day, whether they realize it or not, are blessed by the State of Alaska.

CHAPTER TWO
Fun Facts and Quotable Quotes

"The wilderness needs your whole attention."
— Laura Ingalls Wilder

On January 3, 1959, Alaska became the 49th state of our Union. In so many ways, Alaska stands alone — no other state is comparable. Here are some fun facts about this incredibly unique land.

1. Alaska means "great land." And indeed it is.

2. Hawaii and Alaska are the only two states that are not bordered by any other state.

3. Alaska covers 1/6 of the total area of the United States.

4. Alaska is bigger in area than Texas, California, and Montana combined. (Sorry, Texas. Not everything down there is bigger.)

5. Anchorage, Alaska, is the fourth largest city in area in all of the United States. This one city is larger than Rhode Island!

6. Alaska has six times as many pilots per capita as the rest of the nation combined.

7. Alaska has an estimated 100,000 glaciers.

8. Alaska and Russia are only 55 miles apart.

9. The letters in the name *Alaska* can be typed on the same row of the keyboard. This is true of none other of our states.

10. Alaska pays its residents to live there permanently! The payment to its residents is made from the investment earnings on Alaskan mineral royalties. The payments fluctuate yearly. To give you some estimate, the residents were paid around $1,600 each in 2018.

11. Alaska does not have a sales tax. This is true of only four other states: Delaware, Montana, Oregon, and New Hampshire.

12. Alaska is home to the largest fishing industry in the United States. About 15 percent of rural Alaskans work in this industry.

13. The only World War II battle fought on American soil happened in Alaska (1943 when Japan invaded the Aleutian Islands).

14. On January 23, 1971, the coldest temperature ever recorded in the history of Alaska occurred in Prospect Creek, north of Fairbanks. The thermometer hit 80 degrees below zero.

15. Alaska is the only state where you will find polar bears.

16. The ptarmigan, the state bird of Alaska, has the ability to change its plumage from light brown in summer to snow white in winter. (I enjoyed hunting and partaking of this delicious bird during my time in St. Mary's.)

17. Dog mushing was declared the official state sport in 1971.

18. Barrow, the northernmost city in the United States, has two months of continuous darkness in the winter and three months of continuous sunlight in the summer.

19. Alaskan people invented the kayak for hunting on the sea.

20. A traditional native dessert of Alaska is Akutaq, an "ice cream" made from lard, cooked fish, and berries. (Sounds gross but it is actually quite delicious!)

As you might guess, such a unique state has spawned some interesting quotes over the years. Here are a few of my favorites:

"To the lover of wilderness, Alaska is one of the most wonderful countries in the world." – **John Muir**

"Alaska's beauty is unrivaled – it's a visual feast that takes your breath away and captivates you to the core." – **Tom Bodett**

"Moose are the squirrels of Alaska." – **Tim Moon, Comedian**

"Historically, Alaska is a place that has attracted those fed up with conventionality." – **Bill O'Reilly**

"Nobody is accidentally in Alaska. The people who are in Alaska are there because they choose to be, so they've sort of got a real frontier ethic. The people are incredibly friendly, interesting, smart people – but they also stay out of each other's business." – **Marcus Sakey**

"Ain't Texas cute!" — **Any Alaskan who meets a Texan!**

This is a state like no other! If you are ever blessed to visit, you will discover another dozen fun facts and come back with your own quotable quotes.

Alaska just does that to you.

CHAPTER THREE
Alaska's Greatest Treasure

"It is good people who make good places."— Anna Sewell

You cannot read up on Alaska without discovering a phenomenon known as the Alaskan gold rush. Seward helped make Alaska part of America, but gold made Americans part of Alaska.

After the purchase of Alaska in 1867, few Americans cared to settle there. That all changed thirty years later when gold was discovered. This sparked the Klondike Gold Rush (or Yukon Gold Rush) in 1896. Over 100,000 people from all walks of life left their homes and headed to Alaska and Canada in hopes of striking it rich. The newspapers fed the fever with many articles claiming that gold nuggets "the size of your fists" were just lying in the creek beds waiting to be gathered. Americans, as well as people around the world, got caught up in the rush for riches. Fewer than half of those who attempted the trip made it to the gold fields. Most who arrived stood little chance of finding gold. Most had no idea how to mine and were ill-equipped to do so if they did. Just a handful left as millionaires, most left broke and broken, and many died trying to get there or get back out.

But a few not only made it — they stayed.

The gold rush brought to Alaska what it needed the most — people! Wild, working, wonderful people from all backgrounds, ethnicities and creeds. And the people brought life.

Gold mining is still big today. While visiting Fairbanks, I met young men who work in gold mines. There are currently four gold mining operations in the state; three underground and one open-pit. In addition, there are over 200 placer mines (gold extracted from stream beds). Today, Alaska remains the hub of gold exploration and mining, with new deposits being discovered and developed. From 1880 to 2022, total gold production stands at 54 million troy ounces.

So, is gold Alaska's greatest treasure? I vote "no." The greatest treasure I discovered in Alaska was its people. Many of the lessons I learned while visiting there came from the words and the ways of these amazing last frontier residents.

Alaska is a quilt fibered with an array of coarse threads — from the plain-spoken and prickly to the humble humanitarians; from the strong, quiet natives to the loud, lovable locals. Weave in the miners, the military, and the missionaries, and then stitch generously a vast array of the weird, the wild, and the wilderness wanderers and you get this warm blanket of humanity. And if you stay the winter, believe me, you will need that blanket!

This land has a way of weeding out the weak. You must be tough — physically, mentally, and emotionally — to survive. Alaska bends for no one. You will learn to bend to her, or you will break.

One life-long resident explained it this way: "The Alaskan wilderness is a Jekyll and Hyde. It will lull you to sleep with its majestic beauty and then kill you in your sleep! Enjoy the sights, march courageously into its grandeur, but never underestimate it."

Alaskan people learn a way of life that is foreign to most of us. For seven to nine months every year, you are dealing with cold, inclement weather. That is why you hear this spoken often — "Task, not time." In order to accomplish tasks, you have to accept that most will take more time than it would elsewhere. The weather from above, the winds all around, and even the tundra below your feet will heave and ho in its fight against you. Everything is harder. Patience here is not just a virtue, it is a survival necessity. Slow and steady wins the race, but understand, most of the races are run in muck boots.

I'm not trying to put all Alaskans on the same pedestal. Sadly, you will find the same laziness, same addiction problems, same self-entitlement, same welfare mentality that you find in many of the other parts of our country. As long as our government continues to punish the productive and reward the lazy, these people will exist.

But if you like a challenge, Alaska might be for you. But be warned: you must work hard, be smart, self-sufficient, and savvy. You should be willing to help those around you, knowing that sooner or later you also will need some help. You must be able to handle watching the sun rise only to see it set a few hours later — and then watch the opposite happen six months later. And there's one more thing that might help you make it in Alaska. It might not hurt if you are a little bit crazy — yes, come to think of it, that actually might help a lot!

There is still Alaskan gold. I know, because I found it. You can too if you look. It exists in the hearts and character of its people.

CHAPTER FOUR

The Churches of Alaska

"Stop playing church and start loving Christ." — J. Vernon McGee

My trips to Alaska have always revolved around ministry. As I have already shared, I preached in five different churches on my first trip to Alaska. I pastor an Independent Baptist church in rural Indiana. I cannot speak to the state of all churches of all stripes in Alaska, but the Independent Baptist churches that I visited impressed me. I would go so far as to say that some of the greatest churches in America are in the state of Alaska. And there are some lessons that our churches in the lower 48 should learn from them.

Same but different. Most Independent Baptist churches in Alaska are conservative in their music, traditional in their fundamental beliefs, and consistent in their use of the King James Bible. All cherish the preaching and teaching of the Word of God and all are heavily invested in supporting missionaries. That's where the similarities end. I found different song books, different ministry outreaches and different congregational personalities.

The pastors of these churches come from a vast array of Bible colleges and backgrounds. They were influenced by different men and different ministries. It was nice to see that men of God in Alaska are not instantly judged by where they attended college or what IFB camp they came from, but are instead judged simply on how faithful they are to the Word of God.

How did these pastors end up in Alaska? Some had previously served on a foreign mission field. One pastor, who has been in Alaska for almost 50 years, grew up in Boston, Massachusetts. A missionary couple who serves in a remote Yupik village on the Yukon River claim Florida as their childhood home. Imagine — Florida to Alaska! One pastor left Greene County, Indiana, as a young man back in the '70s and has served for five decades in Alaska. This is the same Southern Indiana county where I now pastor. Because of this, he and his wife are especially dear to me.

Supportive of one another. Despite some differences, the churches root for each other in Alaska. They travel great distances to support each other's meetings. They pray for each other, check on each other, and encourage each other. I never heard a bad word from the mouth of an Alaskan pastor about another preacher near him.

One dear pastor in Fairbanks told me this: "There's not enough of us up here to divide into camps. We have to stick together!"

Doug Cassel pastors a church four miles down the road from me. He is one of my dearest friends. We stand for all of the same things because we both stand with the Bible. Our churches are different in many ways — his has ministries I do not have and vice versa. That being said, we root for each other, pray for each other and support each other. Pastors, missionaries, and evangelists who come to our area marvel at our close relationship. One said, "You two should write a book on how to pastor in the same area and get along!" I thought he was kidding. He affirmed that he was not. "Most pastors have nothing good to say about other churches of like faith in their community, and most despise the other pastors around them."

If that is true, shame on us. Gentlemen, we're on the same team. Maybe it's time we started acting like it.

Missions minded. Many of the churches in Alaska were started as missionary outreaches. Maybe that is why they have such a high commitment to missions giving. One church in Alaska has given over a million dollars a year to missions for the past 12 years running.

My country preacher dad used to tell me, "Son, one of the marks of a great church is a great missions program. God always blesses a church that has a heart to reach the whole world for Christ."

Generous and gracious congregations. There are two things that never cease to amaze me: the grace of God and the generosity of God's people. The latter is especially true of Alaskan churches. Some of the kindest gestures and most generous love gifts that I have ever received have come from Alaskan churches.

Patient and prayerful outreaches. When it comes to evangelism, Alaska has its challenges. It is populated with people who are not easy to reach for Christ.

Years ago, I asked Pastor Tim Page a question. He is the former Greene County, Indiana, resident who went to Alaska 50 years ago as a missionary.

"Brother Page, what did you have to learn about ministering in Alaska that was different from ministering in Indiana?"

He leaned forward and explained to me that it took him about five years to figure out whom he was trying to reach. Then, with a twinkle in his eye, he explained the five reasons people move to Alaska — and being a preacher, he had alliterated the list!

1. *Revenue* — Chasing the high paying jobs available.
2. *Recreation* — To enjoy all things outdoors.
3. *Rat Race* — To avoid the people and pace of the lower 48.
4. *Radicals* — Plenty of hippie, tree-hugger types.
5. *Running from the Law* — Self-explanatory.

Then he leaned in and said, "Imagine trying to invite to church people who are determined to spend their weekends working over-time for double wages; or who want to spend their weekends pursuing their outdoor hobbies; or generally hate people and want to be left alone; or are liberal-minded worshippers of Mother Earth; or who are hiding out from the law behind gates, barbed wire, and posted signs threatening to shoot you if you come onto their property. That's who we are called to reach. Welcome to pastoring in Alaska!"

He then leaned back and laughed. Although what he said was a little tongue-in-cheek, other Alaskan pastors have since affirmed his list to be somewhat accurate.

I might add one more "R" to his list. *Recruited.* There are many military families in Alaska. Some are presently serving while others are retired military men and women who were previously stationed here and just couldn't get Alaska out of their system.

Some of the best Christians that I have ever met are men and women with military backgrounds. Jesus recruited disciples and He is still looking for men and women who will pay the price to be disciples.

Matthew 16:24, Then said Jesus unto his disciples, If any man will come after me, let him deny himself, and take up his cross, and follow me.

The word *disciple* comes from the same word as *discipline.* The best Christians are the most disciplined Christians. Jesus listed the requirements for discipleship. Someone must be willing to deny self, take up a cross, and follow Christ. Compare that to the chief sins of today: selfishness, laziness, and rebellion.

Why do military veterans make great Christians? Because while they served their country, they learned to put a greater cause above their own personal desires. They learned to embrace hardship and follow orders. When a soldier gets saved, it is natural for him to take that same discipline he learned in the military and apply it to his Christian life. The concepts of sacrifice, honor, duty, loyalty — these are not just words to our veterans. They are a way of life. When these traits are focused toward God and His work, the potential good is limitless.

There are a lot of lessons that I learned from attending the churches of Alaska and from spending time with their pastors. I was challenged by their dedication and motivated to go home and serve God with a higher level of devotion.

I might even try to be a little more kind to Doug Cassel... then again... nah!

CHAPTER FIVE

Wolf Pelts

"The aim of life was meat. Life itself was meat. Life lived on life."
— Jack London, *White Fang*

On my first trip to Alaska, I decided that I would like to bring home one keepsake — something that I would never have a chance to acquire in Indiana. I wanted to bring home an Alaskan wolf pelt.

While in Anchorage, I visited the Alaska Fur Exchange. This is an amazing store that is described online as "...unique, carrying fur hats and pelts, soapstone carvings, moose antlers and other Alaskan items." It truly was one of the most unusual gift shops that I have ever visited. Plus, I was excited because they also had wolf pelts for sale.

What I experienced next is what some call "sticker shock." They wanted between $800—$1,200 per pelt. Well, that made me take a step back and wonder if I should settle for a souvenir keychain instead! I didn't begrudge them the price — if I went to the effort the Alaskan trappers do in acquiring these pelts, I would want to be paid a premium also. But the price was out of my range.

We were scheduled to take a jump flight up to Fairbanks later in the week, so I called a friend up there and told him what I was looking for. He told me of a couple of trappers who run a tannery in Fairbanks.

"We'll call Al and Neal. When I pick you up at the airport, we'll go by Al's place and see if he has one that he would sell you."

Either way, to have the chance to tour an Alaskan tannery was exciting. And it did not disappoint.

The first thing I noticed when I pulled into his place of business was a metal sign on the front entrance with a clear message in bright, bold, red capital letters: LEAVE FOUL LANGUAGE OUTSIDE. I had to laugh. Both Al and Neal are Christians, and there were some things they weren't going to tolerate. If you were asked to leave because of your filthy mouth, you couldn't say you weren't warned!

Walking around the shop and seeing firsthand the scores of different projects scattered about was an outdoorsman's dream. Every game animal from across Alaska was represented in that shop. Hoops of pelts hung from the ceiling: fox, wolverine, beaver, mink, arctic fox, lynx, martin, river otter, coyote, and yes, Alaskan wolf. In addition there were moose hides being tanned as well as elk and caribou. The horns and antlers of these same animals were everywhere. A large brown bear hide hung center stage. It was like no place you would ever find in the lower 48.

As fascinating as it was, the part I enjoyed the most was getting to meet Al and Neal. I appreciate the time they took to show us around, answer our questions, and share their trapping stories.

Al and Neal both trap up on the Livengood River, north of Fairbanks. They spend a couple of months each winter, traveling by snow machine between two remote cabins, trapping a variety of fur-bearing animals. They also trap for wolves.

A wolf pelt was the reason I had come, so I was interested in how they trapped them. Al explained that he usually caught the wolves in wire snares. He would pick a thicket where the pack would visit to hunt rabbits, and he would scatter a dozen or more wire snare loops head-high in hopes that a wolf would be snared. He explained that trapping wolves wasn't easy, because they are extremely smart.

I asked, "Have you ever caught more than one at a time?"

"Yes."

"What was the most you have ever caught in one thicket?" He told me that once he had caught five wolves, but that was rare. He explained how it happened.

"Most of the time you just catch one, because the minute he starts yelping the others shoot out of the thicket. You might catch one more as they are fleeing. But every great once in a while, you catch the alpha male — the leader of the pack. When that happens, the other wolves don't know what to do so they will run in and out of the thicket. I caught five that day because I caught the leader first."

I couldn't help but think of how hard the devil goes after those in leadership positions — especially fathers and pastors. If the devil can snare the leader, he will also destroy a lot of the followers.

Al sold me a couple of wolf hides. They hang in my shop and when I look at them, I often think of the four young wolves who were snared because the leader of the pack let his guard down.

Then I ask God to keep me alert, because with leadership comes great responsibility.

CHAPTER SIX
The Steps of a Good Man

"The steps of a good man are ordered by the LORD." — Psalm 37:23

My second trip to Alaska came by invitation to preach at a Christian Men's Retreat scheduled in March of 2021. I was pleased to share the pulpit with Pastor Mike Johnson from Redding, California. The retreat was held at Victory Bible Camp located in Wasilla, about an hour north of Anchorage. Doug Cassel accompanied me on this trip and for three days we had the privilege of rubbing shoulders with Christian men from all over Alaska — missionaries, pastors, church staff, laymen, and teenage young men. I enjoyed every second of it.

I brought to Alaska a box full of knifemaking materials — from the raw metal and wood to the finished product. (Although I stowed it in my check-in luggage, I was not surprised to see that the TSA had opened it for inspection!) I have dabbled in knifemaking for the last seven years and, being a preacher, soon noticed the spiritual correlations. God didn't get much when He saved us, but He can take some raw materials and turn them into a usable tool. For three days I talked with the men about the process — from cutting to grinding, from the fire to the anvil, then back into the fire for quenching. The knife then goes into the oven; then more grinding, polishing, and sharpening. The final step: putting on a handle that fits well in HIS hand. It was a blessed time and God met with us.

Every time we had a meal, I would sit at a different table. I wanted to meet as many men as possible. I would always introduce myself and then point to each one in turn and ask the same question.

"How long have you lived in Alaska and what brought you here? Tell me your story."

I met men from varied backgrounds and all walks of life. A few were life-long residents, but most had been drawn to this wonderful state from elsewhere. I met retired military men, oil-field workers, business men, employees of the large gold mines, and hunting guides. Many were into various outdoor hobbies — trappers, hunters, fishermen — and it seemed that a snow machine (what we call a snowmobile) was a standard necessity. I enjoyed talking to two retired men who actively panned for gold. It was fascinating to hear their stories.

19

Every man has a story of his life's journey — a testimony. As we get older and look back, it is amazing to see how God's hand has led each of us every step of the way.

In addition to the three sessions I taught on knifemaking, I was also asked to preach three other services. At the end of the last preaching service, a young man sought me out. He wore a leather cowboy hat and addressed me as "Mister Pastor Jerry Ross." He was a humble, respectful young man and I sensed that what he needed to tell me was intensely important to him.

"What can I help you with?"

"Pastor Ross, I don't want to bother you, but I need you to know something. While you were preaching tonight, God called me into the Gospel ministry. I know He wants me to be a preacher."

I firmly grasped his hand and looked him hard in the eyes. "What's your name, young man?"

"Jubal."

"Jubal, the ministry is not a game. The call to preach is serious and sacred. If God has really called you to preach, you understand that this is for the rest of your life. No turning back, no turning away. Are you sure of your calling?"

He met my stare, sincere, serious. "Yes, sir."

I prayed with him, rejoiced with him, and then asked him if he had told his father. I had seen the two of them together earlier in the week and had eaten lunch with them. He told me he had not.

I was thrilled to listen to him tell his father of God's call upon his life. Jubal's parents are missionaries to St. Mary's, Alaska, up near the Yukon River in a remote, western part of the state. They would be the reason for my fifth trip to Alaska. But that story is for later.

As I watched Jubal walk away, I wondered what God had in store for this young man. Where would God's will take him? What will his story be? I also thought back on my own life's journey — my story. I remembered surrendering to preach in 1979 and how the call of God forever changed the direction of my life. I thought of how blessed I have been to have my steps ordered by the Lord. I had no idea back then that I would be allowed to preach in 40 of our 50 states.

And I thought how glad I was that God allowed Alaska to be one of those 40.

CHAPTER SEVEN

Uniquely Fairbanks

"Welcome to real Alaska!" — Pastor Doug Duffet

The retreat ended Saturday at noon, then we drove six hours north to Fairbanks. The church that organized the Alaskan Men's Retreat was located there and their pastor had extended an invitation for Doug and me to preach for him on Sunday. I was excited that this trip would allow me to further explore this unique northern city.

In 1901, E. T. Barnette, a banker and riverboat captain, constructed a trading post on the Chena River. A year later, gold was discovered and hundreds of miners migrated to the region causing a boom in construction. In 1903, Fairbanks was officially incorporated. Fast forward to 2020 and the US census now puts the population of the city at 32,515 and the Fairbanks North Star Borough at 95,655.

The residents of Fairbanks love their city and are more than ready to welcome you to "real Alaska". There definitely are some things you will experience in Alaska's second largest city that you will not down on the southern road system. For one, Fairbanks' climate is subarctic producing long cold winters and short cool summers. July is their warmest month with an average high temperature of 72 degrees. January is the coldest with an average low temperature of minus 13 degrees. The coldest temperature ever recorded in Fairbanks was 66 degrees below zero! Residents live under 24 hours of daylight for over 70 days each summer. On the winter solstice (December 21st, the shortest day of the year) there are only 4 hours of daylight. The greater Fairbanks area is a great place to view the *Aurora Borealis* or Northern Lights (best between August and April each year).

Sunday morning after the retreat, Doug and I were blessed to preach at the Bible Baptist Church of Fairbanks. Their pastor, Doug Duffet, arrived in Fairbanks 50 years ago from Boston, Massachusetts. The church has given over a million dollars annually to support missionaries around the globe, and has done so for the last 12 years. A man who is a member there walked up to me after the service and handed me the ball of a woolly mammoth femur bone! He had carved a cave into one side of it with the likeness of a woolly mammoth standing inside the cave. It was masterfully done.

"I heard you were coming, and I appreciate pastors. Here, this gift is for you." Then he smiled and walked away. His name was Chuck, a humble, talented man who embodies the church's generosity and giving spirit. It was one of the nicest gifts I have ever been given and I cherish it to this day.

If you ever make it to Fairbanks, there are some places which reflect the uniqueness of the city — places I consider "must sees."

Mark Knapp's Custom Knives: Mark was a winning contestant on the TV show, *Forged in Fire* (2017, Season 4, Episode 20) and a true craftsman. His shop is a treasure chest of Alaskan hand-crafted souvenirs and you will enjoy visiting with him and his wife, Angel.

Iron & Wood Gun Shop: What makes this gun store unique is the number of vintage firearms they offer for sale. You'll find a knowledgeable owner and a friendly staff — it's like stepping back in time.

*Fairbanks Fur Tannery: Housed in a historic airplane hangar, this business is a definite must see. I purchased a couple of wolf pelts from Al as well as a #9 four-spring wolf trap that his friend, Neal, built by hand.

World Ice Art Championship: This is the largest ice art competition on the globe. It is held at the Tanana Valley Fairgrounds each February and March. Ice carvers from around the world come to compete and their creations stay on display till the end of March.

Alaska Trappers Association's Spring Fling: This is still on my checklist of events to attend, so I cannot speak from personal experience. Held in Fairbanks during March of each year, the ATA celebrated its 50th anniversary in 2024. A trappers auction is held on Saturday and Sunday afternoons and a banquet on Saturday night. I hope to attend this at some point down the road.

The Northern Lights: No words can describe their beauty and no photograph can capture it. This is God's creation at its finest, delicately displaying His handiwork.

Of the five trips I have taken to Alaska, four of them have included some time in Fairbanks. I hope my other Alaskan friends are not offended, but I have to echo the sentiments of the Fairbanks residents — while in Alaska, visit "real Alaska."

*Sadly, during the writing of this book, Fairbanks Fur Tannery was totally destroyed by fire. A time-capsule lost. Prayers for Al and Neal.

CHAPTER EIGHT
I Sought For a Man Among Them

"You have to be a man before you can be a gentleman."
— John Wayne

Before I left Fairbanks, I was invited back to preach again at the men's retreat the following year. I was excited that another trip to Alaska was now on the calendar — I also did not want to return alone.

So on my third trip (March 2022), I invited 13 men to come with me. For all of them, it was their first trip to Alaska and I wanted to experience it with them. Four of them were members of my church, one was a pastor from Montana, and two were a pastor and his son from Rhode Island. Pastor Jonathan Ryser from Princeton, Indiana, also brought his two sons and three other men from his church.

It is hard to put into words the importance of Christian men getting together from time to time at a retreat like this. I know all of us came back helped and changed. Wives, I know it is a sacrifice for you to send your husbands to attend a men's retreat, but he needs it and I believe you will be the beneficiary. Men come back from these retreats better men, better husbands, and better fathers.

I asked a few of the men to send me comments about what God did in their hearts during our time in Alaska. Here is a sampling:

V. Loveless: *"The beauty and vastness of Alaska is enough to prove how great our Creator is. I don't know a better place to prepare a man's heart to hear from God."*

J. Daffron: *"I was greatly encouraged on our trip to Alaska. I was able to see the grandeur of the snow covered mountains and the lights of the Aurora Borealis and everything in between. The Lord used a preacher to preach on the different types of dogs! During this message, I was encouraged to stay faithful to God no matter what life brings my way."*

L. Hall: *"God used the men's retreat to hit a total reset button in my life spiritually."*

N. Walton: *"Alaska is a BIG state! It was good to meet with other men — we are not alone in trying to serve the Lord. Every-*

one of us can be better for the Lord than we are."

P. Chapman, Jr.: *"It was very encouraging seeing so many men of God singing and praising the Lord together. It made me feel less alone. During the week, with God's help, I nailed down where I was supposed to go to Bible college. I left there feeling like a great weight had been lifted off my shoulders."*

Pastor D. Loewen: *"Looking at a room filled with Christian men is a wonderful sight to behold. The potential for Christ is tremendous and the exhortation was clear: 'Be a man!' Every man has pressure and problems, but we cannot run away from our responsibility of being men. There is nothing like a meeting with men in a primitive region like Alaska to send this much needed message."*

In 2012, I wrote a book entitled *Biblical Masculinity*. I did so in response to a growing trend. When I would ask pastors and youth pastors about the state of the young men in our country, I would often receive the same general observation.

"Young men are becoming more and more effeminate. They are increasingly soft. Few are willing to embrace hardship of any kind."

Within a few years of the book's publication, the transgender movement kicked into high gear. I could never have imagined that young men would be confused about their gender — that they would not know which bathroom they were supposed to use!

Christian fathers, grandfathers, and pastors need to rise up against the unbiblical and demonic "woke" cancel culture. We have been silent too long. God made two genders. The Bible is clear on this. We need to once again rear our young men to be masculine, hard working, tough, and resilient. The attack on masculinity is an attack against Biblical Christianity.

The Bible teaches us that it takes iron to sharpen iron. If young men are to grow up into who God wants them to be, they must be properly influenced by masculine men. I would encourage every man reading this book to begin to take the time to influence the young men in your family, in your community, and in your church.

Because, if we don't, the devil has an army of perverts, pansies, and woke politicians who will.

CHAPTER NINE
"I Hurt it Picking"

"Mine eye affecteth mine heart..." — Lamentations 3:51

During the men's retreat, I sat down at a table for lunch with a group of men. I recognized one of them. It was Jubal's dad, Israel Warren — only this year, his arm was in a sling. He and his family are missionaries to St. Mary's, a small Yupik village just off the Yukon River on the far west side of Alaska.

I inquired about his wife and family, then asked the obvious question. "How did you hurt your arm?"

He paused, took a bite of food, chewed, swallowed, then said, "I hurt it picking." Then he proceeded to change the subject.

"Wait. Picking? What are you talking about?"

Again a pause. Then the story came out. A few weeks before the men's retreat, six teenagers in a nearby village made a suicide pact. They all followed through with it on the same night. Israel heard about it and went over to help the men of the village dig the graves.

"This time of year, the frozen tundra is like concrete. We would build a fire to thaw it some, then you have to use a pick to chip out the first four feet of tundra. After that, you can use a shovel. It was slow, hard work and I messed up my shoulder in the process."

I had heard that suicide was a major problem in the remote villages of Alaska. By remote, I mean villages that can only be accessed by boat or airplane. Statistics are one thing, but sitting across from a missionary that had just helped dig six graves made it real. Every once in a while, you have a "God moment." I had never been to St. Mary's, obviously didn't know any of these teens, but my heart became so heavy. What set of circumstances could bring six teenagers to the place where self-inflicted death seemed better than living out their lives? I needed to understand more about what this missionary family was facing and see if there was some way my church could help.

I spent a great deal of time during that meal asking Israel questions — getting his story and trying to understand his mission field. And I wanted to know how God had brought them there.

Israel and Rebecca Warren moved to St. Mary's, Alaska, in

2016. They are blessed with three children: Jubal, Kezia, and Nathan. You might remember that their son, Jubal, surrendered to preach during the first men's retreat.

On the last day of the retreat, Israel approached me with a proposition. "Every fall, I have a revival meeting and try to bring in a preacher that I think could really help our people." Then he paused, looking a little embarrassed. "Of course, we are missionaries and there are not a whole lot of extra funds..."

I held up my hand and stopped him. "First of all, I would be honored to come. Secondly, I pastor a church that has a heart for missionaries. They encourage me to go to the mission field from time to time to serve alongside a missionary family. I know they would be glad to pick up the expense of the trip."

We compared calendars and decided that September of 2023 would work for both of us. I was instantly excited. There was so much about ministering in remote Alaska that I wanted to better understand. He also told me that he would be taking a short furlough during the winter of 2023. I booked him for a meeting in February and we have since taken them on for support.

Another trip to Alaska was now on the calendar.

Before we said our goodbyes, he made me an offer. "Pastor Ross, I have read your book, *Mountain Lessons*, and I know you like to hunt. Although I cannot pay you to come, if you want to bring your rifle, moose season will be in. I think I can put you on a bull moose while you are there."

Wait. What? A moose hunt in remote Alaska? The dream hunt on the top of every big game hunter's list?

He went on. "The area around St. Mary's is among the best parts of Alaska to hunt mature moose. I can't guarantee you a trophy, but if you can stay an extra couple of days, we should be able to find a decent bull."

I had to pause and think about it... for about a half a second!

Thank you, Jesus!

CHAPTER TEN

Wife's Turn

"I hit the wife lottery!" — Jerry Ross

For the handful of women who are reading this book, by now you are probably thinking, "Three trips to Alaska and no mention of your wife? Now you are planning your fourth trip? Are you serious?" Yep, guilty as charged. The first time I tagged along with an evangelist friend, the second with a pastor friend, and the third with 11 men to a men's retreat. St. Mary's would need to be my fifth trip. It was *way* past time to bring my wife to Alaska! My next trip needed to include her. When and how was the question.

I have to thank Pastor Terry McGovern for helping to make this fourth trip happen. He pastors the Independent Baptist Church in Anchorage. The McGoverns served as missionaries to Papua New Guinea for 12 years before accepting the pastorate there in Anchorage. During the opening week of 2022, I received a call from him.

"Brother Ross, every year we bring up a preacher to preach for us from the lower 48. Do you have any Sunday this summer that you could give me?"

I told him I would check and get back with him. I wasn't sure I could do it, because every week of the summer I either had something going on at our church, or I was booked to preach out. As I looked at my calendar, I saw that I had saved the week of our 38th wedding anniversary in July. *(Marriage Tip: NEVER schedule to be out of town preaching on your anniversary! Did that once... ONLY ONCE!)* I called Pastor McGovern back.

"Hey, Preacher, does it matter to you when we fly in and out? My wife and I have an anniversary in July and if we could spend some extra days in Alaska together, it would be wonderful."

He was thrilled that their church could be a blessing and make this happen for us. I got off the phone and called my wife.

"I think I have an anniversary trip planned for us this year."

Silence, then, "I thought we were just going to stay close to home and celebrate here. Where are we going?"

Dramatic pause. "How about Alaska?"

"We can't afford that."

"No, but God can!" And then I explained what happened.

I want to say a word here to Christian young people who are believing the lie that the devil is peddling to your generation. Satan will whisper to you, "Don't surrender to the ministry! If you become a missionary or a preacher, you will never get to do anything fun. You are going to miss out on life!"

That is so far from the truth. First of all, the ministry is fun! The most fascinating and fulfilling life is one dedicated to serving our Saviour. Secondly, if you are willing to sacrifice your dreams for His will, it will amaze you how many different ways God will reward you.

Matthew 6:33, But seek ye first the kingdom of God, and his righteousness; and all these things shall be added unto you.

Psalm 37:4, Delight thyself also in the LORD; and he shall give thee the desires of thine heart.

Don't ever feel sorry for those of us who are serving the Lord. Feel sorry for those who chose their own will over the will of God — eternity will someday reveal what they missed out on.

My wife was excited about God's gift to us. We were able to schedule nine days in Alaska. Every trip you take with your wife includes three phases of enjoyment: planning the trip, experiencing the trip together, and reliving memories of the trip. We enjoyed all three.

We mapped out a plan of how to spend our time there. There was much of Alaska I had not experienced and I wanted to see some of these places for the first time with my wife. Kodiak Island and Seward were two destinations we both voted for.

Of the nine days, we spent two with the McGoverns. They were so kind to us when we were there. They even planned an anniversary fellowship after their Sunday evening service. Again, I was amazed at the generosity of an Alaskan church. I especially enjoyed going out to eat with them and hearing stories of the years they spent in Papua New Guinea as missionaries.

Whatever God calls you to do will require a measure of sacrifice. Carrying a cross comes with being a disciple. But again, the good outweighs the bad, and even the "bad" God masterfully works together for good. So, choose God and His will for your life!

You won't be sorry.

CHAPTER ELEVEN

Kodiak Island

"Kodiak bears are the largest bears in the world."
— Alaska Department of Fish and Game

Sheryl and I are empty-nesters, so we can travel pretty cheaply. Peanut butter and jelly sandwiches are still just fine, and cereal still makes the best breakfast — especially if it is Cap'n Crunch! Our plan was to conserve as much money as possible so that we could splurge on one big event. I wanted to take her to view the brown bears on Kodiak Island.

It worked out to be the right time of the year for it. The salmon were running, so the bears were on the rivers gorging on this annual all-you-can-eat seafood buffet.

Kodiak Bears are a unique subspecies of the brown or grizzly bear. A large male (boar) can stand over 10 feet tall when on his hind legs and 5 feet tall on all four legs. He can weigh up to 1,500 pounds. The females (sows) are about 20% smaller than the males.

There are about 3,500 Kodiak bears — a density of about 0.7 bears per square mile. On the island, they enjoy pristine habitat and well managed fish populations. Cubs are born in the den during January and February, weighing less than a pound at birth with little hair and closed eyes. They suckle for several months, emerging from the den in May and June when they weigh about 15-20 pounds. The typical litter size is two to three cubs.

We landed in Anchorage early on a Tuesday, then caught a jump flight to Kodiak Island where we stayed till Thursday evening. On Wednesday morning we met Rolan Ruoss of Sea Hawk Air. Rolan has been operating a float plane since 1979, and was our guide to Kodiak Island. He is highly skilled and knowledgeable in all things Kodiak — a delightful host and excellent pilot.

Our flight across the island was incredible. We had never been in a float plane, and taking off and landing on the water was amazing. Rolan took the time to point out many of the key geographical sites as we flew and answered our many questions.

We landed in a bay near a river where the bears were known

to fish. A mile hike was required to get to where we needed to go. Once there, we situated ourselves on a slight hillside and spent a couple of hours viewing the bears below. At any given time there were about 20-30 Kodiak bears feeding below. Most were 60-100 yards away, but some wandered closer. At one point, a sow with two cubs camped about 40 yards from us. I was a bit nervous, but Rolan assured us that we were fine.

"As long as we don't approach them, they tend to just ignore us. There has only been one person killed by a bear on Kodiak in the past 75 years." About the time he was explaining this to me, one cub ran toward us up the hill and got within 15 yards before circling back to its momma. The sow stood up and looked our way, and I thought there was a chance we would triple the number of human casualties!

Sheryl and I brought binoculars, and the two hours went by quickly as we watched the bears feed and frolic. The salmon bravely fought their way through the gauntlet of bears, most making it past, but a few becoming bear snacks.

Rolan explained the amazing life cycle of the salmon.

"Eggs are laid and hatched in fresh water streams and lakes. The 'smolts' then live near where they are hatched for 1-2 years. Then they move downstream into the freshwater bay where they continue to grow before eventually swimming into the saltwater ocean. The ocean is their home for 1-3 years as they grow to full maturity. Then comes the amazing part: something triggers them to begin the journey back toward the place where they were born. They do not eat on this journey, living off stored fat reserves. Swimming relentlessly upstream, they return to the place they were born, lay their eggs, spawn, and die. Then the cycle begins again."

As he spoke, I pondered the greatness of our Creator. It is impossible to overstate the importance of salmon as a food source for mankind. Imagine a fish that can adapt from freshwater to saltwater, then back again; a fish that can live in the vastness of the Pacific Ocean and yet find its way back to the exact stream or lake where it was born. The atheists will come up with an array of theories — any theory will work in their minds as long as it excludes the existence of God.

As Sheryl and I watched the Kodiak bears catch these home-travelers, we did not feel closer to Mother Earth, or have the desire to go hug a tree. We did sit in awe at the greatness of our Creator.

We hiked back to our plane, enjoyed a simple lunch, then soon were lifting off as the float plane skidded across the water.

Rolan circled the island offering us incredible views. Kodiak Island is home to the Kodiak National Wildlife Refuge, a 1.9 million-acre sanctuary on Kodiak and Afognak Islands. It was established in 1941 by President Franklin D. Roosevelt, "for the purpose of protecting the natural feeding and breeding range of the Kodiak Bear." The brown bears are among six mammals indigenous to the Kodiak region. The others are foxes, river otters, short-tailed weasels, bats, and tundra voles. Later, humans introduced Sitka black-tailed deer, mountain goats, reindeer, snowshoe hares, beavers and red squirrels.

It is legal to hunt Kodiak bears. Hunters will kill about 180 bears each year under tightly controlled regulations. This helps maintain a healthy bear population. About 5,000 resident hunters apply annually for a chance at 490 bear permits. About 70% of Kodiak bears killed by hunters are males. Nonresident hunters must hire a professional guide. The cost? Anywhere between $10,000 to $20,000.

Our pilot eventually landed us back outside the city of Kodiak. Our plan was to enjoy a nice supper, have a relaxing evening, then explore the city the next day.

The city of Kodiak has a population of 5,581 (2020 census), making it the 10th largest city in Alaska. Commercial fishing is the mainstay of its economy as well as tourism, mainly by those seeking hunting and fishing adventures. The harbor was crowded with fishing boats of all kinds offering us postcard quality views. The city was simplistic but stunning. We ate a light breakfast and then began our self-guided walking tour.

A visit to the city's museums gave us a look back into the history of the Island. Both the Alutiiq Museum and the Kodiak History Museum were well worth the small entrance fees. Also, the Kodiak National Wildlife Refuge Visitor Center was fun to tour. After that, we visited a few shops, grabbed a light lunch, then returned to the hotel to rest.

The visit to Kodiak Island was wonderful, but what made it next level was having Sheryl along. During the week we were in Alaska, we celebrated our 38th wedding anniversary. We have tried to center our lives around the Lord first, and each other second. I cannot begin to put into words how blessed I am to have her. I hit the wife lottery and I know it! We have served the Lord together since the day we were married — we are a team. On everything I have ever done that has succeeded, you will find my wife's fingerprints somewhere. If you have been blessed with a good Christian wife, then make sure she knows that she is appreciated, cherished, and valued.

Too soon, our time on Kodiak Island was over, and we took the jump flight back to Anchorage. We still scroll through the pictures that we took while we were there, reliving the memories and wondering at the goodness of God.

CHAPTER TWELVE

Seward

"I will not believe that thou hast tasted of the honey of the gospel if thou canst eat it all to thyself." — Charles Spurgeon

We returned to Anchorage on Friday, then spent the weekend ministering at the Independent Baptist Church in Anchorage. We enjoyed our time with Pastor Terry McGovern and his wife, Mariann. The church is vibrant, sweet-spirited, and active in evangelism and discipleship. The people were receptive and responsive to the messages.

Monday, our plan was to drive the two and a half hours to Seward, Alaska, and spend the day. Our schedule did not allow it, but there is a train, the Coastal Classic operated by Alaska Railroad, that runs between Anchorage and Seward. It is four hours each way and promises, "some of the most scenic miles of rail in the state." They also provide onboard dining as well as narration by host tour guides. Had we the time, we would have liked to experience Alaska this way.

There were two main reasons I wished to visit Seward. One was an invitation I had received from a young man who was getting ordained into the Gospel ministry. He heard I was going to be in Alaska and asked me to come serve on his ordination council. I was honored to have a part.

Secondly, I wanted to visit Scott Johnson. I met Scott at one of the men's retreats. He introduced himself in an unusual way.

"Hello, Pastor Ross. My name is Scott. They took an offering for the guest preachers last night and I had left my wallet in the cabin. Instead of giving towards that offering, I will send you something in the mail."

I thanked him and, to be honest, forgot about it until I received an insulated box in the mail a few weeks later at my home in Indiana. Scott and his wife had sent me a box full of freshly caught salmon and halibut packed in dry ice. There were also fresh moose backstrap steaks included! My wife and I couldn't get over this kind gesture.

I called Scott to thank him and in our conversation learned more about the ministry he oversees in Seward. The Alaska Christian Mission to Seafarers (ACMS) is a ministry to the crews of the many

33

cruise ships that dock yearly at Seward. The ministry provides free transportation from the ships to the mission where guests are gifted free Wi-Fi access, home cooked meals, and a safe environment to relax and refresh. The mission's main goal is to share the gospel of Jesus Christ with the cruise ship personnel. Most of these ship employees are from third–world countries. The mission fields of the world literally come to the Seafarers' Mission each summer (people from 85 different countries in 2023). It was great to meet up with him, spend time at the mission, and meet his wonderful staff.

Sheryl and I spent a couple of hours exploring Seward, enjoying a little R&R (to my wife, that stands for restaurants and retail). We then attended the ordination service for the young man entering the ministry. This was held at the Resurrection Bay Baptist Church on the south edge of Seward by the bay.

One of the greatest blessings of my life is to watch young men surrendering to the Gospel ministry. I often say, "At my age, it sure is encouraging to look in the rear view mirror and see an army of young preachers stepping up and stepping out!"

At the end of the service, as we had a time of prayer for this young couple, I asked the Lord to continue to raise up a new generation of Bible preachers. If you are a young man, my prayer is that you would be open to the call of God upon your life. I understand that it is not God's will for every young man to be a preacher, but in every generation, the Lord calls young men into His service. If He calls you, be willing! Run to it, not from it.

Romans 10:13-15, *For whosoever shall call upon the name of the Lord shall be saved. How then shall they call on him in whom they have not believed? and how shall they believe in him of whom they have not heard?* ***and how shall they hear without a preacher?*** *And how shall they preach, except they be sent? as it is written, How beautiful are the feet of them that preach the gospel of peace, and bring glad tidings of good things!*

At the end of our time in Seward, we drove the two and a half hours back to Anchorage. Our hearts were full. No matter where you go in this world, God has His people. It sure was encouraging to see that the Gospel Light was shining bright in Seward.

CHAPTER THIRTEEN
An Inconvenient Diagnosis

"Beloved, think it not strange concerning the fiery trial which is to try you, as though some strange thing happened unto you:" — I Peter 4:12

During this fourth trip to Alaska, I began to experience some abdominal pain. It was hard for me to sleep at night and the pain began to intensify. I told my wife that I had better get checked out by my doctor when I got back home.

Years ago, a man in my church was diagnosed with what proved to be a terminal illness. I drove him back and forth to receive treatments, and on one of those trips he offered me some sage advice.

"Preacher, your body will talk to you if you'll listen to it."

Well, it was time for me to listen. Long story short, after a PET scan, I was diagnosed in August of 2022 with non-Hodgkin lymphoma, more specifically, diffuse large B-cell lymphoma (DLBCL). Lymphoma is a cancer of your lymph node system.

Yikes! No one wants to hear the "C word".

Cancer is no respecter of persons. Almost everyone reading this has a family member who has had to deal with cancer. Some of us have lost loved ones to this terrible disease.

Both of us felt like we had been struck by lightning. But in the days that followed, God quickly gave us a peace that truly passed "all understanding." If it was God's will that this be part of our journey, then we determined to face it together, maintain our faith in God, and do our best to bring Him glory.

What I am going to say next will only be understood by avid hunters — but as I was going over the treatment plan with my doctor, in the back of my head I was thinking, "I'm scheduled to be with Israel in the fall of 2023 to do missions work and go moose hunting. This better not mess that up!"

Between my diagnosis in August of 2022, and my next scheduled trip to Alaska in September of 2023, I underwent a number of different treatments.

Six chemo treatments each spaced 21 days apart.

Simultaneously, six chemo injections into my spinal column.

After that, 25 radiation treatments, 5 per week for 5 weeks.

Then in May of 2023, they recommended I have a CAR T blood transplant. To do this, they extract from you a type of white blood cell called "T cells". They then ship them to Salt Lake City to "weaponize them" so that when they are reintroduced into your body, they will attack your cancer cells. Before they do this you have to go through three days of intense chemotherapy.

Three days of chemo.

T Cell transplant.

11 days in the hospital.

3 weeks in isolation staying within 10 minutes of the hospital.

By the time I got home, it was the middle of June. It would take till the first of November to see whether the CAR T treatment did any good. I returned home with a greatly compromised immune system and only about 30% of my original strength and stamina. It was an uphill battle as I began to work my way back to my previous normal.

I tell you all of this because some of you are facing challenges in life — maybe health, maybe something else. Maybe you can't do what you used to be able to do. Discouragement sets in and, if you're not careful, you will just give in to it.

Don't. Don't quit. Don't quit trying. Push yourself to do more than you think you can. Prove the doctors wrong. Ask the Lord for strength, then play the man. **Play the man!** A week after I got home, I began preaching every service at my church.

I kept in touch with Israel. I told him that, Lord willing, I would be there. It helped having something on the calendar to work towards. I had three months to build myself back up physically so that I could pull off this trip to remote Alaska. I could lie around and feel sorry for myself, or I could get to work.

My mother's life verse was Philippians 4:13: *I can do all things through Christ which strengtheneth me.* Every one of us can do more than we think we can. One man said, "When you ask God to move a mountain, don't be surprised if He hands you a shovel." Pray for strength, set some goals, push yourself, and watch what happens.

Eighty-eight days after arriving home from the hospital, I boarded a plane for St. Mary's, Alaska.

CHAPTER FOURTEEN
St. Mary's

"This is no time for ease and comfort. It is time to dare and endure."
— Winston Churchill

A late night flight into Anchorage was followed the next morning with an early flight into St. Mary's. The plane that services St. Mary's is a Beechcraft 1900, a twin-engine turboprop regional aircraft that accommodates 19 passengers, their gear, and whatever freight comes along for the ride. It also delivers the mail to St. Mary's for the USPS. Because we were in the middle of moose season, most of the passengers aboard the flight were hunters.

For those used to landing in modern airports, St. Mary's is a step back in time. Climbing out of the plane, you step onto the tarmac and sink into an inch of mud. The concourse is a large metal pole-barn type structure, the baggage claim is a row of pallets along the runway fence, and your luggage is delivered via a large diesel Caterpillar front-loader. There to greet me were Israel, his children, and one of Jubal's friends, Ricco. It was about noon on a Friday when I landed. We loaded my gear, and drove the short distance to St. Mary's.

As we neared the village, Israel took a short detour that took us to the top of a small hill, affording us a view of St. Mary's. There was also a small cemetery there. It was the right place to start my time there — looking past the cemetery to view the village was a reminder of why this family was there; of why I was there. Someone needed to bring the Gospel to these people. For hundreds of years people here have lived and died, and for much of that time, no one was there to tell them of a loving God who sent His Son to die for their sins. I felt something stir inside of me, and whispered a prayer that we would see souls saved during the next nine days.

The 2021 census tells us that 602 people live in St. Mary's. There are two more smaller villages that are connected by roadway — Mountain Village and Pitka's Point. In addition to ministering to these three villages, the Warrens use the Yukon River as a means to reach other remote villages. They boat to these villages until the winter freeze, then use the river as a highway for their snowmachines. Occasionally, Israel's brother-in-law, Job, will fly his bush plane over to St.

Mary's to take Israel to a village that is only accessible by plane. While I was writing this chapter, I received this text from Israel:

"Just flew into the village of Marshall, upriver 50 miles, to do a funeral. Young man went missing a month ago. Found him floating under thin ice 4 days ago. Warm fall, early winter. River still too sketchy to snowmachine on."

A simple text from a missionary in remote Alaska, yet it provides a window into the circumstances they face and the means they must use to minister to the people who need them.

Israel drove me around the village, giving me a quick tour before heading to their home and church. They are housed in the same building as the church, a 120′x30′ building divided into two parts. Both are too small — they have packed a family of five into a small apartment on one end and are packing a growing congregation into a small auditorium on the other end. The goal is to build the Warrens a house, giving the church the entire present building. I determined to help in some way and paused to pray that God would lead others to give generously toward this need.

Because of the cancer treatments, I had only regained about 75% of my strength and stamina. I had slept four hours in the previous 25 hours, so I needed to rest a bit. Upon arriving at their home, I settled into a small Sunday school room on the church side of their building, and slept on an air mattress for the next couple of hours.

Brother Warren told me, "Preacher, see how you feel when you get up. We might want to give a go at putting you on a moose later this afternoon." Needless to say, I was excited about the chance to go hunting on my first day in St. Mary's. I didn't think I'd be able to fall asleep, but once I laid down, fatigue quickly set in and I slept hard.

But before falling asleep, I spent some time praying. I asked God to help me to be an encouragement to the Warrens and to be a blessing to the people of St. Mary's.

CHAPTER FIFTEEN

Moose Hunting

"Hunting teaches us patience, humility, and respect for the natural world. It's a way of life built on principles." — Jim Shockey

By four o'clock in the afternoon, I was loading my hunting gear into Israel's boat. Soon, four of us — myself, Israel, Jubal, and his friend Ricco — were headed down the Andreafsky River, toward the mighty Yukon. I had to pinch myself. To be boating on the Yukon, heading out to hunt moose in remote Alaska — well, most big game hunters will never get this opportunity. This was a dream come true.

An hour later Israel steered us into a tributary that fed into the Yukon. After a couple of miles, the creek forked, then began to narrow. Israel idled down the outboard, and we began to look in earnest for moose. He ran the boat up a couple of sloughs, and spent some time calling, to see if we could get a bull to respond. Finally, we grounded the boat and set out on foot into an area of open tundra that had produced bulls in the past. We had spent about a half hour walking and glassing when Israel spotted the massive horns of a bull moose who was bedded down about 800 yards out.

He handed me the binoculars. "Look where I am pointing. When he moves his head, the sun is reflecting off his horns. He looks like a good one." After talking it over, we decided to make a stalk and close the distance. We were walking into a left-to-right cross wind, so we knew we had a chance to get on him. The only downside was the direction we were walking — it was angling us away from the river.

We closed the distance to 600 yards, and from there we could get a much better look at him. There was a small lake between the bull moose and where we stood, which meant we had to veer either left or right. If we went left, he would wind us. Right would take us even farther from the river. Israel began smacking a boat oar against some brush to see if we could get him to come to us. The bull stood up, irritated, but refused to come our way. Now we could see him much better.

"He's a good one, Preacher. Probably mid-60s." Moose horns are measured by the greatest distance between the outside edge of each horn. A 65" moose is a nice bull. We watched him for some time, trying to decide if we could get to him with the time we had left before sunset. "It's your call, Preacher. But if we take him, we will spend this evening and all day tomorrow packing him out. He is a good half-mile from the river."

A half-mile through the tundra is not easy. Saturday evening was the first night of the revival so we didn't have a lot of time to deal with a moose. But he was a monster! I was definitely torn.

About that time, Israel's phone buzzed. It was Jubal texting us. He and Ricco had spotted a nice bull not far off the river, just about 75 yards from where we had left the boat. They estimated him to be close to 60 inches. I looked one more time at the mid-60s bull, then made up my mind.

"Let's hike back to where the boys are and take that moose. I want to stay focused on ministry while I'm here, and that will be a much easier pack-out." He nodded in agreement, glad for my decision.

We hoofed it back toward the boat and soon joined Jubal and Ricco. They pointed out the bull. It was herding four cows toward the willows along the river. We were about 200 yards away, the wind was right, and there was cover between, so we decided to close the distance. After a fast trot, we eased out of the brush and there stood the bull moose. My range finder registered 135 yards, and the bull had not spotted us. Israel told me he thought the bull was around 55 inches. Not the monster we left behind, but still a good bull.

Using the boat oar as a rest, I shot the moose twice through the lungs. It took two steps and stopped. Israel told me to keep shooting till he was down. I shot several more times — the last thing we wanted was for him to run into the tundra away from the river.

This moose was tough! But my .300 Win Mag did its job. I cannot tell you how excited I was to have taken my first bull moose.

We had left Israel's house at 4 PM. By 7:30 PM, I was standing over a 52.5" Yukon bull moose. God was certainly good to us! I had been blessed to see two nice bulls, and to harvest one on my first evening at St. Mary's. I did not regret passing on the larger bull. The bull I took was close to the river so it would be an easy pack-out. We could get it done and still be ready for the Saturday evening service.

I have to give a shout-out to Jubal and Ricco. Had it not been for them, we would not have seen this trophy. It was a great hunt and a forever memory with good friends.

CHAPTER SIXTEEN

The Work of the Ministry

"Whosoever will be great among you, let him be your minister."
— Jesus Christ

We field dressed my moose as the sun was setting, then tarped it and hiked to the boat. All we could do was pray that a brown bear didn't make a midnight snack out of it. The boat ride back was incredible and we arrived home tired and hungry but so excited for what God had allowed us to accomplish.

One of the men who attends Israel's church is a federal conservation officer by the name of Matt. When he heard that I had "caught" a moose (a term used in Alaska that makes me smile), he volunteered to help us pack out the meat. I have great admiration for the men and women who serve their communities as COs. Yes, part of their job is to enforce the hunting and fishing regulations of their state, but most of their time is spent in true service — search, rescue, and assisting those in need. The fact that he took the time to help us pack out my moose meant a lot.

Even though we were in close proximity to the boat, it still took several hours to pack out the meat. Jubal brought a couple of his friends — Ricco and Daylon — and I sure appreciate how hard those young men worked. The Bible tells us that "the glory of a young man is his strength" and I was thankful for their help.

It is hard to appreciate the size of these beautiful, majestic animals until you walk up on one. Israel estimated the moose to weigh around 1,400 pounds. It yielded over 600 pounds of good lean meat.

My goal was to take the horns home with me, and about 40 pounds of meat. The rest would help feed the Warren family through the winter as well as provide meat for the elders of the village. I was excited that we would be able to be a blessing to some of the Yupik folks who were too old to be able to hunt or fish.

Israel reminded me of something I needed to hear. When we discuss ministry, we think of preaching, evangelism or discipleship. Ministry in its purest form is serving others. I was amazed at how much of the Warrens time is spent in assisting those who simply need a helping hand. Yes, taking meat to some elderly residents was *minis-*

try. That week, I watched Israel and his family serve others — by helping an elderly couple mount a WiFi antenna on their house, by boating out to take a battery to a stranded hunter, and by helping a village teenager get his four-wheeler started. They also make sure people have the firewood they need and help many with home maintenance.

Helping others, serving others — that is ministry.

I do not believe that good works gets a man to heaven. But after someone is saved — after he receives Jesus as his personal Saviour — he is called to good works.

Jesus spoke these words to His disciples: *"Ye are the light of the world… Let your light so shine before men, that they may see your good works, and glorify your Father which is in heaven."* (Matthew 5:14-16)

Good works are your light! This requires us to have a servant's heart — to look for opportunities to bestow good works upon others, and then to make sure that the glory goes to our Heavenly Father. Yes, I was excited to be able to take a bull moose, but the main reason for that excitement was not so that I would have a set of horns to hang on my wall, but for the opportunity it would give us to minister to those who needed the meat.

My parents did not get saved till they were 26 years of age. Dad had bought a small mini-farm north of Brazil, Indiana, and moved our family there from the Greencastle area. Living across the road from us was a Christian couple about the same age as my parents. Jerry and Ruth Purcell and their two boys were good neighbors. They always looked for opportunities to lend a hand. I remember Jerry coming home from work after a long 12-hour shift, setting his lunch bucket on the hood of his truck and then walking across the road to help us get our hay in the barn before the rain came in.

The Purcells eventually got my parents to come to church with them. My dad and mom heard the gospel and got saved. Because of that, our entire family was transformed. Why was my dad willing to listen to Jerry Purcell? Why did they have influence in our lives?

Ministry.

Yes, always be ready to hand someone a gospel tract. But be just as ready to help someone put up their hay.

CHAPTER SEVENTEEN

Trophy Hunts

"For the Son of man is come to seek and to save that which was lost."
— Jesus Christ

On my flight up to St. Mary's, the majority of the other 18 passengers on our plane were hunters. Every one of them boarded that plane with a dream. All hoped to reboard it with a giant moose rack packed away in the hold. Several were serious trophy hunters who had invested over $20,000 for the chance to take a monster moose.

Spending my life around hunters has taught me something. What may be a trophy to one may not be to another. I have seen an experienced whitetail hunter disappointed when his blood trail ended with a 140 inch rack — a buck he thought was 150+ when he released the arrow. I have also watched a young boy wipe tears of joy over a fork horn. I give the same piece of advice to all hunters — take what makes you happy. Don't worry about what everyone else thinks.

I sat among them praying for my own trophy, one that I doubt any other person on that plane would understand.

Revival meetings started on Saturday night at *the* Faith Baptist Church there in St. Mary's. I was so excited to see the small meeting room packed out. The Yupik people who attended were warm and welcoming and I was impressed at their excitement. Israel had preached for weeks and had their hearts prepared and praying for revival. God gave me liberty and we had a wonderful first night.

The meeting resumed on Sunday night, and God led me to preach on the rapture — the soon coming of our Lord Jesus Christ. Two Yupik men — one a middle-aged man and one a teenager — raised their hands during the invitation indicating that they were not saved. Right after the service, I sat down beside the adult man and talked to him about the Lord. His name was Peter.

He shared some things with me that were personal — things he had struggled with for years. I was moved by his honesty and could definitely see the Lord was working in his heart. God allowed me to open the Bible and help him with these things and then the subject turned to salvation. He knew he was not saved and knew he needed Christ. A short time later, he bowed his head and called out to God for forgiveness and salvation. He was excited to share this with Israel and with Jezreel, the man who had invited him to church.

The next night, God moved again in the service and the teen-age young man who raised his hand on Sunday responded again. I asked his parents after the service if I could talk to him about salvation. They both were excited and tearfully urged me to talk to their son, Jez-mond. I found out later that they had only been saved a short time themselves.

I spoke with Jezmond for some time, carefully explaining the Gospel. It was obvious that he had been sitting under good preaching and that God had prepared his heart for this moment. Jezmond too was sweetly saved. God had heard my prayer for a trophy and had answered twofold.

Later in the week, Israel would help me build a crate and care-fully pack my moose horns for the flight down to Anchorage. Once there, I uncrated them, then wrapped them in bubble wrap. I placed plastic pipe over each tine, then placed a sleeping bag over each side. Then I shrink-wrapped the entire thing. I was going to have to trust my horns to some Alaska Airlines baggage handlers and I was going to make it as hard as possible for them to destroy my prize. After the shrink-wrap, several rolls of packaging tape was used to secure it all.

The day I flew out of Anchorage for Indianapolis, I carted my luggage and horns through the Anchorage Airport. I thought it would turn some heads. Hardly anyone noticed. Seems like this happens a lot during this time of year in Alaska! I checked the horns with my checked baggage, then boarded the plane first for Seattle, then from there to Indianapolis.

I stood beside the oversize luggage conveyor belt in Indy, pray-ing my horns would come out in one piece. I breathed a sigh of relief when they arrived unscathed. When I picked them up and slung them over my shoulder, EVERYONE in Indianapolis stopped and stared. Ap-parently this doesn't happen every day in Indiana!

That moose rack is hanging over my fireplace at home, but it is not my Alaskan trophy. Leading Peter and Jezmond to Christ will al-ways be my greatest memory of that trip.

1 Thessalonians 2:19-20, For what is our hope, or joy, or crown of rejoicing? Are not even ye in the presence of our Lord Jesus Christ at his coming? For ye are our glory and joy.

CHAPTER EIGHTEEN

The Yupik People

"If your heart were sincere and upright, every person
would be unto you a looking-glass of life." — Thomas à Kempis

I live in Greene County, Indiana. Our county demographics state that we are 96% Caucasian. I have lived here on, then off, then back on again for 35 years. Let me tell you about white, southern Indiana people. There are some really good people here, and there are a handful of really bad ones. Most are hardworking but we have our share of shiftless, lazy people. Some are racist, some are not. Drugs and alcohol are both a problem where I live. Crime happens. We have registered sex offenders residing in our county. Sadly, "bad people" get too much attention and too much press. Most people here are good, honest, and family-oriented, and many are still God-fearing.

People are people the world over. We all have the same problem and that is sin. The cure is also the same whether it's in Jasonville, Indiana, or St. Mary's, Alaska. Jesus is the cure.

I found the same variety of people among the Yupiks. Most I met were good people. They welcomed me and treated me kindly.

Are drugs and alcohol a problem? Of course. But there are also many hardworking, honest men and women who have moved to St. Mary's because they want a good life for their children. The school is excellent and attracts many quality teachers and educators.

The people of St. Mary's are good natured — they laugh easily and enjoy good humor. This is a village that could become the prototype of what a successful Alaskan remote village could and should be. But I believe that this will never happen without God's help. In the next chapter we will deal very honestly with the darkness that hovers over St. Mary's. But this chapter is about its citizens: the Yupik people.

I could delve into their history. I could tell you who they are historically and culturally. I could make some broad-brush statements that might contain elements of truth. But that would be wrong. If I tried to buttonhole everyone into a broad category where I live in Southern Indiana, it would be unfair. If you want to know about us — the people of Jasonville — I would say to you, "Come meet us. Because we are as varied as the unlimited design of our Great Creator."

Who are the Yupik people? If pressed, I would speak of Jezreel and his love for the Lord and hunger to learn the Bible. I would tell of his dear wife, Janelle, and their two bundles of energy, Samson and Titan. I would tell you of Ricco and Daylon, two young men who have surrendered to preach the Gospel and are on fire for the Lord. I would tell you of Peter, a combat Marine veteran who attended the service and accepted Jesus as his Saviour. I would introduce you to Paula and her husband, Arthur, whom I so enjoyed talking to and were so kind to bring me parting gifts. I wish you could meet Charlie and Jewelleeann, the new converts whose son, Jesmond, got saved on Tuesday night.

Who are the Yupik people? Gordon and Mary Sallison, elders who started praying in 1986 that someone would come to St. Mary's and start a Gospel-preaching church (1986 was the year Israel was born!). There are many other faithful folks who attend the church there: Walky and Bay; sweet Marian; Dale and Mary Ellen and Justin and DeeDee. Some are retired while others work at various jobs in the village — some at the airport, others for the City or State; some at the Public School, or the Commercial Store or for the local tribe. These are good people with hopes and dreams, strengths and weaknesses, good days and bad, just like the rest of us.

And I can't leave out Rudy, a Yupik man who is three years younger than me, and because of that, calls me *grandpa!* In return, I call him *grandson.* And we both do so in fun. Who would have believed I had a grandson in St. Mary's?

But mostly, I would tell you of the need for families like the Warrens — Israel, his wife Rebecca, Jubal, Kezia, and Nathan. Because without missionary families to go to these difficult places, there would be no light — only darkness. Sin is the problem but Jesus is the cure! And I thank God someone is pointing them to the Light of the World.

Who are these people? My answer is simple: they are my friends. At the end of the week when my plane lifted off the runway, I began to miss them. I gave them a part of my heart, and many were generous enough to give me a part of theirs in return.

CHAPTER NINETEEN
The Darkness

"It is better to light a candle than curse the darkness."
— Eleanor Roosevelt

When I had met Israel at the second men's retreat. He had been wearing an arm sling because he had damaged his shoulder digging graves for six teenagers who had carried out a suicide pact.

The morning I flew into St. Mary's, Israel shared with me some grim news. A sixteen-year-old young man had hung himself behind the local high school on the playground equipment. His name was Tyron.

The family was required to fly his body down to Anchorage for an autopsy. This takes several days, but halfway through my visit we were told that the body had returned and the family was preparing for a three-day wake. Israel and I went to the home to pay our respects. Tyron was laid out on the floor of the family home on a pallet, and the loved ones and friends were gathered around. I knelt beside the grieving mother, introduced myself, then asked her to tell me some good memories of her son. She wept as she talked about her "baby". We prayed with the family, ate at their table, sat awhile, then left. The mother told me as we left, "You can come back anytime you like."

Remote Alaskan suicide statistics will give you cold facts. But visiting Tyron's home put faces to this ongoing tragedy.

I believe that St. Mary's has the potential to become a prosperous and successful remote Alaskan village. I also believe that this will never happen unless a supernatural war is fought and won. You see, St. Mary's is a satanic stronghold. And the evil one does not surrender his territories easily.

Yes, in St. Mary's there are extended times of physical darkness. The shortest day every year, December 21st, measures only 5 hours and 15 minutes between sunrise and sunset. By the way, this does have a real effect on the people who live there. Even Christians struggle during the months of 15-19 hours of daily darkness.

But the real darkness is a Satanic cloud that hovers over the remote villages. Drugs and alcohol are widely abused. Heinous crimes are too frequently committed, and many of them go unpunished.

There are generational sins that permeate some families — sexual sins that seem to be too easily accepted and excused as normal. No young girl or young boy ought to ever hear her or his mother say, "It happens to everyone. You just need to get over it."

A dark despair permeates the young people — a hopelessness driving some of them to self-destructive behavior and even suicide.

Israel told me that there are three types of remote villages: dead, dying, and living. He told me that the dead and dying villages need to do just that — they need to and will eventually die. These are small villages of just a handful of people, populated by those hiding from the law, sexual deviants, and social outcasts. Any family who wants to give their children any chance of a decent life are fleeing these villages and going to a "living" village. Thankfully, two-thirds of remote villages are living villages. These are villages where the majority of people want a good school, job opportunities, and a safe environment to rear their families. Of the 250 remote villages, Israel feels there are 160 living ones—and each needs a Gospel-preaching church.

St. Mary's is a living village and because of that it is growing. Population numbers reflect this: the 1990 population was 441; in 2000 it was 500; in 2010 it hit 507 and by 2018, the population was estimated at 567. In 2022 the village topped the six hundred mark with 602 residents. The Warrens are able to minister to four villages within 26 miles of their home.

Please understand, this does not mean that villages like St. Mary's have escaped the satanic hold of this region. Spiritual darkness still exists. Some of the sins of the dead villages still find their way in.

The last night I spent in St. Mary's, I was sound asleep in a SS classroom when I heard Israel enter the church and call my name. He told me to get up and load my Glock. As I was doing so he explained.

"A native man who is prone to violence is drunk. He has already assaulted two women, raping and beating them. One is non-responsive. He has made threats against my family. We are probably not in danger, but we best be ready."

This is the darkness that I am speaking of. The Warrens minister there every day. Yet they stay. Because someone must shine the light. If St. Mary's is ever to rid itself of this spiritual darkness, it will only happen through the power of the Gospel of Jesus Christ.

Who has the courage to go to the other 156 villages?

CHAPTER TWENTY

A Wednesday Night Charge

"How shall they hear without a preacher?" — Romans 10:14

The revival in St. Mary's ran from Saturday to Wednesday evening. Israel had a special service planned for the closing night. His son, Jubal, and two of the Yupik teenage young men have surrendered to preach. He wanted me to give these young men a charge concerning the ministry. This wasn't an ordination service, just a service designed to encourage the young men to stay committed to their calling.

I was especially honored to preach this service for two reasons. First, Jubal had surrendered to preach two years earlier under my preaching. Secondly, Ricco and Daylon were the first Yupik young men ever to have surrendered to preach. This was huge!

How do we reach the remote villages of Alaska? What is the Bible plan for evangelizing any people group? The answer is simple: we must win, disciple, and train them to reach their own people.

It is doubtful that we will ever have enough people from the lower forty-eight surrender to be missionaries to Alaska. Don't get me wrong, one of my prayers for this book is that it would providentially find its way into the hands of some young man whom God would call to Alaska. But it is doubtful that we will have the 60 preachers that we need to come north to evangelize the remote villages. So, what is the answer? The answer is young men like Ricco and Daylon. The answer is Yupik men and women reaching their own people for Christ.

I preached from II Timothy, chapter 4. I exhorted these young men to be true to their calling. I warned them that the devil was going to fight against them doing so. Afterwards we had prayer for these young men, and then Israel presented each a *Strong's Concordance* and an *1828 Webster's Dictionary*. He now meets regularly with them teaching them how to study the Bible and how to prepare sermons.

Foreign missionaries and native preachers — we need both to reach Alaska for Christ.

I hope I have not painted remote Alaska as an easy mission field. It is not. I think the Warrens have been uniquely prepared by God to be able to minister in this "off the grid" location. What does it take to be a missionary in a third-world country atmosphere?

A specific call of God. When times get tough, what is going to keep you on the field is knowing without a doubt that it was God who called you there.

A real and consistent walk with God. If your relationship with the Lord is not real, you will never make it on the mission field.

A strong physical constitution paired with a tough mental determination. You have to be in good health. Some people have a weak physical constitution. If that is you, then you have to be realistic about what the will of God is. But even a strong body must be fortified with mental toughness — you must be determined to fulfill God's will.

The patience of Job. Everything takes longer and everything is harder. Israel often reminded me, "Task, not time." You have to take one job at a time and get it done — and not worry about the clock.

Basic handyman and mechanical skills. There is no repair shop to take your chainsaw or snowmobile to when it breaks down.

Outdoorsman skills. You must hunt or catch most of your own food. Then you must have the ability to process it properly.

A merry heart and a positive attitude. This is medicine for your body and sanity for your mind.

A wife of extraordinary virtues. Israel would not be able to do what he does without Rebecca. She, to me, is the hero of the family. In a remote Alaskan village, she must be a wife, mom, chef, nutritionist, nurse, cheerleader, food forager, school teacher, and chief organizer. Rebecca counsels the ladies of the church, mentors the teenage girls, and mothers all the children. She also is an avid reader and a talented artist.

A missionary wife in remote Alaska must live her life on high alert because of the inherent dangers of living in the village. There are wicked and violent men who live around them. Imagine holding your children at night while a drunk native is trying to kick in the door of your house as he screams aloud the things he is going to do to you and your children. Imagine your husband holding a pistol praying that he does not have to kill this man. This does not happen often, but it has. Could you stay there and try to reach these people for Christ?

I left the village at the end of the week asking God to forgive me for not spending more time praying for our missionaries.

CHAPTER TWENTY-ONE
The Last Frontier

"Jesus answered and said unto him, Verily, verily, I say unto thee, Except a man be born again, he cannot see the kingdom of God."
— John 3:3

The phrase, "last frontier" is defined as "the last region to be discovered, explored or settled by human beings." For many years, you would find the phrase "The Last Frontier" stamped on Alaska's official license plates. From an earthly perspective, of all of our 50 states, Alaska has the greatest right to claim this mantra.

But there is another land that no living American has ever yet explored. The song writer described it like this:

There's a land that is fairer than day,
And by faith we can see it afar.
For the Father waits over the way,
To prepare us a dwelling place there.

Let me ask you a question: If you died right now, do you know 100% for sure that you would go to heaven?

Many will quickly say, "No one can know that for sure!" But the Bible tells us a different story.

1 John 5:11-13, *And this is the record, that God hath given to us eternal life, and this life is in his Son. He that hath the Son hath life; and he that hath not the Son of God hath not life.* ***These things have I written unto you that believe on the name of the Son of God; that ye may know that ye have eternal life,*** *and that ye may believe on the name of the Son of God.*

This portion of Scripture drives home two absolute truths: First, God wants you to know that you have eternal life. Secondly, this certainty is wholly dependent upon you receiving His Son.

Jesus reaffirmed this when he spoke to his disciples.

John 14:6, *Jesus saith unto him, I am the way, the truth, and the life: no man cometh unto the Father, but by me.*

Have you ever received Jesus Christ as your Saviour?

If you have not, you are not alone. No one is born "saved." And everyone who is "saved" was at one time "not saved." What is the difference between someone who goes to heaven when he dies and someone who goes to hell when he dies?

The difference is this: a saved person has received Jesus Christ as Saviour and a lost person has failed to receive Jesus as his Saviour.

Would you like to get saved today? Do you feel God working in your heart right now urging you to make this decision? God loves you and he wants you to be saved today.

First, you must understand that your sin is what is sending you to hell. Heaven is a perfect place and God is a Holy God. Our sin is what is standing between us and heaven.

Romans 3:10 & 23, As it is written, There is none righteous, no, not one… For all have sinned, and come short of the glory of God;

Matthew 13:41-42, The Son of man shall send forth his angels, and they shall gather out of his kingdom all things that offend, and them which do iniquity; And shall cast them into a furnace of fire: there shall be wailing and gnashing of teeth.

Revelation 21:8, But the fearful, and unbelieving, and the abominable, and murderers, and whoremongers, and sorcerers, and idolaters, and all liars, shall have their part in the lake which burneth with fire and brimstone: which is the second death.

The Bible goes so far as to say that even liars shall have their part in the lake of fire. We all have sinned and we all have fallen short of God's righteous standard.

Secondly, you must have a sorrowful and repentant attitude toward your sin. If you feel no conviction about your sin, you are not ready to be saved. A man must come to a place where he is sorry that he is a sinner and truly wants to be cleansed from his sin.

Luke 18:10-14, Two men went up into the temple to pray; the one a Pharisee, and the other a publican. The Pharisee stood and prayed thus with himself, God, I thank thee, that I am not as other men are, extortioners, unjust, adulterers, or even as this publican. I fast twice in the week, I give tithes of all that I possess. And the publican, standing afar off, would not lift up so much as his eyes unto heaven, but smote upon his breast, saying, God be merciful to me a sinner. I tell you, this man went down to his house justified rather than the other: for every one that exalteth himself shall be abased; and he that humbleth himself shall be exalted.

One man in this story thought that he was worthy of heaven because of the good things that he had done. He was so full of pride and self-righteousness that he was unwilling to admit that he was a sinner. The second man did not speak at all about his own goodness, but saw himself as God sees us all, a sinner in need of salvation.

Thirdly, you must understand the Gospel — the good news of Christ's death on the cross in payment of your sins.

1 Corinthians 15:1-4, Moreover, brethren, I declare unto you the gospel which I preached unto you, which also ye have received, and wherein ye stand; By which also ye are saved, if ye keep in memory what I preached unto you, unless ye have believed in vain. For I delivered unto you first of all that which I also received, how that Christ died for our sins according to the scriptures; And that he was buried, and that he rose again the third day according to the scriptures:

Romans 6:23, For the wages of sin is death; but the gift of God is eternal life through Jesus Christ our Lord.

Romans 5:8-9, But God commendeth his love toward us, in that, while we were yet sinners, Christ died for us. Much more then, being now justified by his blood, we shall be saved from wrath through him.

Yes, we are all sinners, and yes, because of our sin we do not deserve to go to heaven. But Jesus Christ loved you so much that He was willing to come down to earth and die for your sins. Your sins have been paid for! Forgiveness is available! Christ purchased for you the gift of eternal life. But you must be willing to receive that gift.

Lastly, you must be willing to put your faith in Jesus Christ and His payment for your sin. And by faith, you must call upon Him.

John 1:11-12, He came unto his own, and his own received him not. But as many as received him, to them gave he power to become the sons of God, even to them that believe on his name:

Romans 10:9, That if thou shalt confess with thy mouth the

Lord Jesus, and shalt believe in thine heart that God hath raised him from the dead, thou shalt be saved.

Romans 10:13, *For whosoever shall call upon the name of the Lord shall be saved.*

Are you ready to be saved? Are you truly sorry for your sins? Do you believe that Jesus died on the cross for your sins, was buried, and rose again the third day? Are you ready to place all of your faith and trust in Jesus and Jesus alone for your salvation?

Why not call out to Jesus right now and ask Him to save you? Pray this prayer to Him right now, and mean it with all of your heart.

"Dear Jesus, forgive my wicked sinfulness. I now put my trust in you and you alone for eternal life. Please save me right now and make me one of Your children. Thank You for saving me! Amen."

I am so happy for your decision. Please reach out to me and let me know that you have accepted Christ as your Saviour.

Pastor Jerry Ross: bhbcpastorjerry@sbcglobal.net

CHAPTER TWENTY-TWO

Wheels Up

"There should be a good in every goodbye." — Unknown

Five different times I have flown out of Alaska. Every time it was with a heart overflowing. Thank you for taking the time to read some of that overflow.

I believe that when you return from any trip that God allows you to take, two things should be true. You should return diminished and you should return replenished.

God has blessed me to be able to travel some as part of my ministry. I always want to leave something behind. Everywhere you go in life, plan on purpose to be a blessing. People ought to have been made better because you spent some of your life with them.

But don't just give out. Take in. A divine Instructor lives inside of every born-again believer. There are lessons the Holy Spirit wants us to learn from whatever situation He allows. Today, there are things He wants to teach you. Every morning, ask Him to guide you, to instruct you, and to give you opportunities to be a blessing to others.

It was not easy saying goodbye the five different times I left the Last Frontier. But one thing helped each time. I have never left without having a plan to return. If my health holds out, I have two trips already planned — one with my wife and one to return to minister again in remote Alaska. Even if the circumstances of life derail those plans, I know that I will see my Alaskan friends again. You see, a Christian really never has to say goodbye. Because of Christ, all my *farewells* have been turned into *see you laters*.

I hope you have enjoyed traveling back and forth to Alaska with me. Even if you never get to visit our 49th state, I hope by reading this book, you feel like you have been. I pray that some of the lessons that I have shared have helped you in some small way.

Pray for the churches of Alaska. Pray for the many missionary pastors who brave the elements to reach people for Christ. Pray for the Warren family and the people of St. Mary's.

And if you are a young man seeking the will of God, take a moment to ask the Lord if Alaska might be the place of His will for you.

Other Books by the Author

Mountain Lessons

Life Lessons Learned While Hunting Elk in the Mountains of Montana

Lake Lessons

Life Lessons Learned While Fishing a Majestic Minnesota Lake

21 Tenets of Biblical Masculinity

Transitioning Young Men From Boyhood to Manhood

Grace Will Lead Me Home

A Vietnam Veteran's Testimony

Stay in the Castle

One Young Lady's Decision to Wait for Her Prince

The Teenage Years of Jesus Christ

The Ultimate Pattern for Teenagers Today

Did God Put a Book Inside of You?

Impacting the Culture Through Christian Writing

104 Bible Lessons, Volume 1

Two Years of Weekly Bible Lessons for Teens & Adults

104 Bible Lessons, Volume 2

Two More Years of Weekly Bible Lessons for Teens & Adults

Additional Resources Available At

Ultimate Goal Publications

Order by phone or online:

812-665-4375   *www.stayinthecastle.com*